MW00947298

This Notebook Belongs To:

____

Made in the USA
Middletown, DE
02 March 2023

26069812R00057